Alt

CW00816291

Adapted by REVD. PETER HAWKINS
from the original text by Bishop Thomas McMahon

FOR USE IN THE ANGLICAN CHURCH

McCrimmons
Great Wakering, Essex, UK

First published in the United Kingdom by
McCRIMMON PUBLISHING CO. LTD.
Great Wakering, Essex, England
info@mccrimmons.com
www.mccrimmons.com

ISBN 978-0-85597-223-3   (13 digit)
ISBN 0-85597-223-8   (Old 10 digit)

ACKNOWLEDGEMENTS

Our grateful thanks to Nicholas Ridge and the Parish Church at Pinner for
their editing and proof reading skills for the revised edition of this book.

The Post-Communion prayer for Maundy Thursday commencing – 'Lord Jesus
Christ, we thank you…' from Common Worship 2000 is © The Archbishop's
Council of the Church of England and is reproduced with permission.

Cover design by Nick Snode
Cover photography: www.iStockPhoto.com
Printed by Index Print, Colchester, Essex, UK   A/AA

Contents

Introduction

This booklet began because I wanted to find something for servers in my parish to use and refer to, in order to help them at the altar. I discovered an excellent booklet by a Roman Catholic priest. Father Thomas McMahon, now Bishop of Brentwood, called *Altar Servers' Missal*; but it needed some adaptation for Anglicans. The opportunity to produce a further edition has enabled me to make further necessary changes, so that it can be used in conjunction with *The Church of England Common Worship Services book (2000)*.

It is a cause for thanksgiving that in one form or another, the Parish Eucharist or Parish Communion has become the main service today in the majority of Anglican parishes. Our Lord's command to 'Do this in memory of me' is being observed now by Anglicans as naturally as it was by the first converts to the faith who 'remained faithful to the teaching of the apostles, to the brotherhood, to the breaking of bread and to the prayers' (Acts 2:42). More frequent celebrations of the Eucharist mean a need for more servers, and servers need guidance. Hence this small book.

Servers will be quite wrong, however, if they expect to find here all he needs to know about serving. The essence of assisting at the altar is to accept that each church will have its own ways, and the server must learn to adapt. None the less, churches (and individuals) can all too often perpetuate their own idiosyncrasies for no good reason other than not knowing what goes on elsewhere. For this reason I hope this publication will be of use.

We need to remember that the offering of the Church's worship is not a matter for the priest assisted by his servers. Worship is an activity of the whole Christian community, and a server must learn that part of his or her task is to break down the barrier between the sanctuary and the people, not to reinforce it. An altar server's role is therefore to make sure that ceremonies are carried out in a devout and orderly manner so that the People of God can recognise themselves to be what they are: a worshipping community. It is not good for the server to be in the sanctuary for every service. It is all too easy for servers to consider themselves quasi-cleric (and robes help this), when in fact they are members of the Christian community called to exercise their gift as a minister of the altar (See: 1 Corinthians 12:4-11).

To be involved with the trivia and details of preparing for worship can easily lead to casualness and frivolity about holy things. This is quite different from real Christian joy, which is what one ought to find in a server who knows that he or she is in fact serving the Lord and Saviour. As servers progress they need to become more and more aware of why they are doing what they are doing. For example, it is a fairly elementary matter to understand something of the meaning of Christ's presence in the Holy Sacrament. But what of Christ's presence in his people, in the scriptures and in the priesthood? Furthermore, what does it mean to see priesthood in terms of the whole people of God and not just of the ministerial priesthood of an ordained man? (1 Peter 2:9)

To pray and ponder these things is to begin to discover the real mystery of the Eucharist. I hear people say that the mystery is lost in modem liturgy. It is only mysteriousness that is lost, not mystery. The mystery of Christ in his sacramental gift to us will take a lifetime of pondering.

I should like to acknowledge my debt to Bishop McMahon. Without his book to adapt I should not have found either the time or the enthusiasm to produce this. He is not, however, to be blamed for any of my errors! Finally I should like to commend *Using Common Worship: Holy Communion* (Mark Beach, CHP 2000), which is recommend to all servers who want to read a straightforward introduction to the presentation of the present liturgy.

Peter Hawkins,
Westbury-on-Trym

Prayers before serving

Go before us, O LORD,
     in this our sacrifice of prayer and praise,
and grant that what we say and sing with our lips
     we may believe in our hearts,
and that what we believe in our hearts
     we may practise and show forth in our daily lives.
Through Christ our LORD.

     Amen.

Prayers after serving

Bless, O LORD, our hearts and minds,
and grant that as we leave your house,
     we may continue to be aware of your presence.
Through Christ our LORD.

     Amen.

The Church year

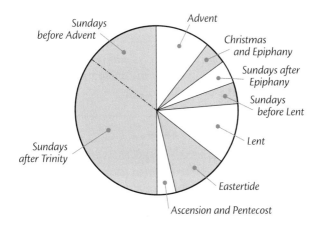

As we know, the calendar year begins on the first day of January. The Church's year however, begins at the end of November with the season we call Advent. This is because the seasons of the Church take us through the life of Christ, from before his birth to the time after his death. As in the calendar year each season has its own beauty – the spring blossom and flowers, the warm summer sunshine, the autumn colours and the beauty of a winter landscape – so too with the seasons of the Church. Each season has its own special beauty and message. Also, like the calendar year, with its ever repeating cycle of birth (spring) and death (autumn), the Church's year speaks of the birth, death and resurrection of the ever-living Christ.

Finally, as one season automatically leads us into another (spring must naturally lead us into summer and not autumn), so, too, one season of the Church automatically leads us into the next. The theme of each Sunday varies according to the season that we are in; and this is why it is important to understand the meaning of each season, so that we can grasp the message that is put across to us as the year unfolds.

✸ Advent

This word comes from the Latin *adventus* and means *coming*. The word was often used in association with the arrival of a king in the Roman empire, or to describe God intervening in human affairs. Advent Sunday marks the start of the Church's year. It embraces four Sundays, and is regarded not just as a period of preparation and reflection for celebrating the birth of Jesus, but also for Christians to be ready and prepared for his return at the second coming.

Some churches have an Advent wreath which, with its four candles, symbolises the four Sundays of Advent and welcomes the approach of the King of Light.

✸ Christmas

This is the second greatest feast of the year and celebrates with great joy the birth of Christ. Like any birthday it is a time of great happiness, and we give and receive presents to show our joy and love. Jesus has come into our world to tell us about God and to show us the way to him.

✸ Epiphany

This is a Greek word which means *appearing* or *showing*. Christ was born as an unknown child in a stable at Bethlehem, but through the three Wise Men who came to seek him, and went back to tell people about him, he was made known to the whole world. It is also known as the 'feast of lights' because of the star that guided them to Christ. We, too, must seek and follow Christ, 'the light of the world', and make him known to others.

✸ Sundays after Epiphany

Easter Sunday is always on the Sunday after the first full moon following the spring equinox on 21st March (the time when the sun crosses the equator). For this reason the date of Easter varies, and so there are a certain number of Sundays which fill in the time after Epiphany. They tell us about the beginning of the public life of Jesus. Common worship has up to nine Sundays after Epiphany, the last three at least being 'Sundays before Lent'.

Lent

This is a time of forty days beginning on Ash Wednesday, and recalls the forty days Jesus spent praying and fasting in the desert. It is marked by sorrow for our sins and some form of penance, to show that we are really trying to live as Christ showed us. It ends with Holy Week, which includes Maundy Thursday when we celebrate the Last Supper, which was the first Eucharist; and Good Friday, when Christ died on the cross. During Lent we do not say the *Glory to God in the highest* or *Alleluia*, so as not to anticipate the joy of Easter.

Easter

This is the greatest feast of the whole year. It is even greater than Christmas, since the fulfilment of something is greater than its beginning. On this day Jesus rose from the dead and promised that we, too, will rise one day. For this reason we no longer see death as the end but as the beginning.

This is why the early Christians changed the day of the sabbath from Saturday to Sunday, and so in this sense every Sunday is a 'little Easter', and so should be a day of great joy and hope.

✳ Ascension and Pentecost

Forty days after Our Lord rose from the dead he returned to the Father. As he had promised to his disciples before he ascended, he sent down the Holy Spirit on them at Pentecost (Whit Sunday). This was a Jewish feast held on the fiftieth day after the Passover (which is what the word means). The Holy Spirit came to renew and strengthen the disciples; and we look upon Pentecost as the commissioning of the Christian Church. The word *spirit* means *breath or life*. The receiving of the Spirit changed their lives and inspired the disciples to go out preaching and teaching about Christ Jesus. This is what should happen in our lives when we receive the Holy Spirit, given to us initially through our Baptism and Confirmation.

✳ Sundays after Trinity

We have now retraced the life of Christ. The Church uses the other Sundays of the year that remain (about thirty in all) to put before us different aspects of his teaching. Each Sunday Eucharist may have a particular theme. We must listen carefully to the Lessons and Gospel, in order to understand what the message is. You will find that the last four Sundays after Trinity are now called Sundays before Advent. It is a time to celebrate and reflect upon the reign of Christ on earth and in heaven, and culminates with the celebration of 'Christ the King', before we prepare for the coming of Christ in the Advent season.

Vestments

Most people today are very clothes conscious. They pay great attention to style and colour. The kind of vestments worn in church, and their colour, have always had a very special meaning. Besides the inner spiritual preparation there is also the outer physical one. The natural feeling that we ought to put on different clothing for divine worship was something people had learnt long ago. There was always a special vestment for the celebrating priest. It was not until city fashion changed to a new shorter costume that liturgical vestments came to be distinguished from ordinary dress. What the priest and server wear now still resembles the costume of ancient Rome.

✸ Cassock

This word comes from the Italian *casacca* and means *great* coat! It was the outer garb of priests and clerics. It used to be worn out of doors instead of a suit, but is now used as a garment for both priests and servers in church.

✸ Surplice or Cotta

This goes over the server's cassock and is a smaller version of the alb which the priest wears for the Eucharist.

✸ Amice

This is a linen cloth with two long tapes, which may be worn to cover the shoulders of the priest or server during the Eucharist. It is an optional garment, and is not worn with the new-style alb.

✸ Alb

A long tunic in linen as worn in the fourth century. Its name comes from the Latin *albus* meaning *white*. Nowadays priests and servers may wear a cassock-alb.

✸ Girdle

A long piece of cord which may be used to secure the cassock or the alb.

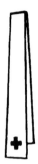

 ## Stole

A very important vestment worn around the neck of the priest. It is thought to come from the silk scarf worn by Roman orators. It is the distinctive mark of order worn by bishops, priests and deacons when celebrating the sacraments. It also signifies their duty to preach the Word of God. You can distinguish between a deacon and a priest because the deacon wears his stole crosswise.

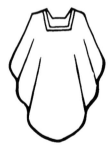

 ## Chasuble

The word means literally a 'little house'. It is the outer garment which covers all the other vestments and its colour changes according to the feast or season. It is the most significant garment for the Eucharist.

✸ Cope

A full vestment in the shape of a
cloak (from which it originated),
sometimes worn by the priest in
processions, and used on occasions
for Evensong and weddings, etc.

Colours of Vestments

In worship we are lifted up to God in various ways by what we
say and do and hear. Another very important way is by what
we can see. In this respect, colour always plays an important
part in our lives. We choose colours carefully to reflect certain
moods.

✸ Purple

These vestments are worn for Advent and Lent.
They express the mood of penance and preparation before
a great feast.

✸ White or gold

These are worn on many important feasts. The colour is a
sign of celebration and joy.

✸ Red

This colour is used at Pentecost, to recall the fire of the Holy Spirit, Palm Sunday, Good Friday and the feasts relating to the Holy Cross. It is also used for feasts of martyrs, since they shed their blood for Christ.

✸ Black

This may be worn for a funeral, although more usually today we wear purple or white, to express our belief in life after death and in the Resurrection.

✸ Green

This is the colour you will see most often on a Sunday. This is because green is the colour of nature and of the new life which shoots forth in the Spring. This reminds us during the Church's year that we are always being given new life to nourish our spirit, as we listen to God's Word at the Eucharist and receive Holy Communion. Green is the colour of hope, and the Christian goes on his pilgrim way full of faith and hope.

✸ Blue

In some churches this is used during Advent instead of purple.

✸ Lenten Array

Unbleached linen or 'sackcloth' is used in some churches in Lent, instead of purple. In these churches all altars will also be covered in the same material to form the Lenten Array.

The sacred vessels

☀ Paten

A circular vessel resembling a flat dish or plate on which the bread is placed during the Eucharist.

☀ Purificator

A folded piece of linen used to purify or cleanse the chalice.

☀ Chalice

The sacred cup used at the Eucharist to contain the wine, as Jesus used at the Last Supper.

※ Corporal

This comes from the Latin *corpus*, meaning a body. It is a square of linen cloth on which the paten holding the sacred Host and the chalice are placed on the altar.

※ Pall

A linen-covered piece of stiff material which may be used to cover the chalice during the Eucharist.

※ Chalice Veil

This is used to cover the chalice and may be white or the same colour as the vestments of the day. It is now optional.

※ Burse

Although the burse is no longer necessarily used, some churches retain it. It comes from the same word as *purse*, and has the same function of holding something. In this case it is used to hold the corporal.

 **Ciborium or Communion Bowl**

A vessel which contains the small hosts for the Communion of the people. In many places a deep paten is used instead of a ciborium.

What to prepare
– In the church –

—✦— **Altar**

Usually the priest will require a book stand or cushion for the altar book. He may also require an altar card.

—✦— **Candles**

A candle is not only useful in so far as it gives light, but it is a wonderful symbol of Christ, who said: 'I am the light of the world'. For both these reasons, candles have been used in worship since the very earliest times.

Lighting a candle can be very difficult. For example, you may not be able to see the top of the candle you are trying to light. It will require patience and care. If there are many candles, begin with the highest (for obvious reasons!) starting near the centre of the altar and working outwards. One point worth remembering, when carrying the candle lighter, is always to hold it with the wick pointing upwards, and not down, and then it won't flare up. If a candle is difficult to light, it may be because the wick is too short, or there may be a surplus of wax around the top which needs clearing away.

When you put the candles out, do take great care not to crush the wick, or it will be very difficult to light next time. Also, take care not to spill wax on the altar cloth or carpet – it is extremely difficult to get off!

—✥— Lectern

It is becoming usual to use a free-standing lectern for all the books and papers required for the first part of the Eucharist. This is often near to the altar; but it may be some distance away. You will need to make sure that the book of readings is in place on the lectern, as well as any card or book the priest may want for the first part of the service. If the Intercession is read from the lectern, make sure any lists needed are to hand. You may also need to provide the priest with a copy of the readings and perhaps other material by his chair.

—✥— Credence table

Before the Eucharist, the chalice and paten with at least purificator, pall and corporal (see pages 20-21) should be set out ready. Other articles that may be required on the credence table include the lavabo bowl and cloth (for washing and wiping the priest's fingers), perhaps a small bell, and the tabernacle or aumbry key (for where the holy Sacrament is reserved). Wine and water and the bread for Holy Communion will be needed unless these are brought to the altar in an offertory procession. If there is to be an offertory procession, make sure the cruets of water and wine and the ciborium with the wafers for Communion are ready on a table in the body of the church.

—⋇— Servers' books

Make sure you have a book which will enable you to follow the service and, most important, to lead the congregation in the responses. For a sung Eucharist it is best to make sure that sufficient books, including hymn books, are in their places for servers beforehand.

—⋇— Hymn numbers

If it is not a choir responsibility, make sure that the right numbers are up on the board and that they are taken down after the service.

—⋇— Alms dishes

Make sure these are ready for those who are responsible for the collection.

─✢─ Acolytes' candles

If separate bases are needed for acolytes' candles or for torches, make sure these are in position before the service.

– *In the sacristy* –

─✢─ Vestments

These should be laid out on the vestment chest in the order the priest needs to put them on. Since the chasuble is put on last of all, it should be put out first. On top of this is placed the stole, then the girdle, followed by the alb, and last of all the amice if one is used (see pages 15-16).

─✢─ Altar books

These should be marked and ready. Make sure you know which books are needed, and check whether the priest needs to find places in them. One of the books may be carried in the entrance procession by a server.

─✦─ **Thurible**

For the occasions on which this is used, the thurifer should prepare the charcoal and see that the incense boat is full. Spare charcoal needs to be at hand. Make sure there is some provision for emptying the thurible safely when you have finished.

─✦─ **Acolytes and torchbearers**

Have the candles and matches ready. Do hold them straight when they are lit so that wax doesn't go all over the floor and never mess about with your candles!

─✦─ **Robes**

It is important to know where your robes are kept, so that you can find them with the minimum of fuss. Whose job is it to keep them clean and laundered? If there is no sacristan for this, make it your responsibility. Older servers please remember how much younger servers need your good example; and new servers need your help, advice and encouragement.

─✦─ **Microphone and lights**

It is very important to see that these are switched on beforehand, so that you don't have to come rushing back and disrupt everything as soon as the service has begun.

Manner of serving at the Eucharist

Here are a few hints and tips. You will find others elsewhere in this book, especially as you follow through the order of the service from page 37. This book makes provision for the needs of servers at a sung Eucharist; by leaving out what does not apply when several servers are present, it can be used for a said Eucharist.

✛ Prayer

There will be opportunities for your own prayers during some parts of the Eucharist (e.g. after Communion), but you should never begin serving without at least a brief prayer of your own, and you should never finish without a thanksgiving. Suitable prayers for you to use in church before and after serving are to be found on page 8.

⊕ Dress

Do arrive in good time and suitably dressed. Remember that your shoes, socks and collar are all likely to show, even though you may be wearing a cassock. Clean hands and finger nails, and tidy hair, are all part of the way you prepare to serve.

⊕ Robes

There is a good case to be made out for servers not being robed. If you are wearing robes it is so that you can help, with the priest, to create the right devotional atmosphere in the sanctuary. Be careful in the way you put your robes on. Try to keep them clean and tidy. Above all, try to deep an atmosphere of quiet calm in the sacristy before the Eucharist begins.

⊕ Standing and moving

Always walk with dignity, keeping your hands joined or clasped unless you are carrying something. Be unhurried. Bow or genuflect with care, so that it is a complete action rather than something cut short. Always stand up straight with both feet firmly on the floor. Never lean on anything!

⊕ Mistakes

You will make them. I remember with embarrassment
bowing to the congregation instead of to the altar the first
time I was in the sanctuary! Disregard a mistake by letting it
pass without drawing attention to it. The chances are that
the priest and congregation won't notice if you don't flap
and don't lose your dignity.

⊕ Paying attention

It is hard not to cough or sneeze. It is even harder not to
yawn if the sermon is boring. But try not to! During the
service, always try to look at where the action is, at the altar,
the lectern or the chair. Do not look at the congregation or
let your gaze wander round the sanctuary.

⊕ Joy

At the same time, do try to look happy! What kind of
advertisement are you for the Christian faith if you cannot
show any joy? The miserable-looking server is no asset in
the sanctuary.

*Common Worship (2000) and the
Revised Common Lectionary (1998)*

These books provide a wealth of material – but it is
sometimes difficult to find your way through them!
Ask your priest to show you where to find what is used in
your church. Every server should possess a copy of these
books.

⊕ Fasting before Communion

In order to approach the Sacrament with reverence, you
should try to have no food or drink (except water) for an
hour before you receive Holy Communion. This is not
intended to be an arduous discipline; it is meant to help you
remember the significance of what you are about to share in.

Here now are some specific instructions/or servers with special duties in the Eucharist, and for parts of the service where something special happens and there is not room to explain in the text that is set out from page 37.

⊕ MC (Master of Ceremonies)

The MC should supervise the preparations for the Eucharist as well as the servers during it. They will be on hand for emergencies and problems before and during the service, but must never be intrusive or fussy. They need to know the service and its structure well.

Once when I was explaining to a group of servers how the priest today needs spontaneity even at the altar, my MC replied: 'That's fine. Father, and I will tidy up after you!' I am not sure what was expected, but that was exactly the right attitude.

Today, as we define the specific tasks of servers less and less, the role of the MC as the one upon whom everyone can depend, who helps everything to run smoothly and without a hitch, and who can gently cope with visiting priests, becomes more and more important. When I hear that an MC is unnecessary in today's liturgy, my reaction is that both priest and liturgy are impoverished without a skilled senior server.

⟶⊕⟵ Crucifer

The crucifer should carry the cross for the procession to
and from the sanctuary. The cross should always be upright,
never pointing forwards, nor held too high. The crucifer
should not attempt to genuflect when carrying the cross;
and if they bow, they should do so modestly without
dipping the cross. This applies also to banner bearers.

⟶⊕⟵ Thurifer

Where incense is used, the thurifer comes to the priest and
raises the lid of the thurible by means of the ring at the top
of the centre chain. They then grasp the chains just above
the lid with the right hand and raise the thurible to the level
of the priest's hands. After the priest has put incense on the
charcoal (and blessed it) the thurifer lowers the thurible
and closes the lid. Should the priest need to take the
thurible, the thurifer passes it to the priest with the right
hand. They receive it back in the left hand as the right hand
is then free to keep it swinging gently.

Incense may be required for the entrance procession (put
incense on in the sacristy), at the beginning of the Eucharist
to cense the altar (optional), for the Gospel, at the offertory,
and for the consecration. For this, and perhaps in a long
procession, the thurifer will need to put on incense himself.

Do be careful. It is a great mistake to try to smoke people
out or to make them or the priest uncomfortable.

—⊕— Acolytes (and torchbearers)

Always remember to keep the outer hand on the middle of
the candle and the other hand on the base if the candle is a
small one. For torches, the outer hand is above the other.
Only bow your head, and not your whole body, or wax will
go all over the floor!

—⊕— Posture

A server should in general stand when the celebrant stands,
and may sit when the celebrant sits. In my view it is never
necessary for a server to kneel during the Eucharist and may
receive Holy Communion standing. But in these matters
you must follow the custom in your local church.

⊕ Procession to the altar

This forms up in the following order (of course not everyone mentioned may be present):

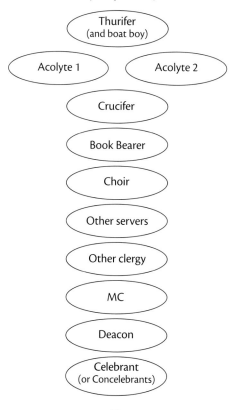

─◈─ **At the altar**

Genuflect or bow together and move slowly to your places.
To genuflect, keep your back straight and head erect as you
go down on the right knee (*genuflect* means to *bend the
knee*). You genuflect when the Blessed Sacrament is in the
sanctuary. Whether the Sacrament is in a tabernacle in the
centre or an aumbry to the side of the altar, there is no need
to genuflect other than at the beginning and the end of the
Eucharist. This is because to turn your attention to the real
presence of Christ in the reserved Sacrament is to direct
attention away from the purpose of the Eucharist itself.
Christ is present through the mystery of the Eucharist.
Should the Sacrament be reserved in an aumbry to the side
of the altar, you should still genuflect.

If the Sacrament is not reserved, you bow to the altar at the
beginning and end of the Eucharist. This should be a low
bow. There is no need to bow other than at the beginning
and end of the service, although the custom of your own
church should be followed.

The Eucharist

The Eucharist is not simply a service conducted by a priest. It is *the* act of worship that Our Lord told his people to do in remembrance of him. Priest and people share together in the offering of the Eucharist. Our part therefore as servers is just as significant as the priest's, although it is different. The way we listen, the way we make the responses, the way we join in the hymns and prayers, the way we stand and sit, should indicate that we take our part seriously. Moreover, we can encourage other members of the congregation by our devotional attitude and by understanding what we are doing.

The basic order of the Eucharist is set out on the next few pages, but can vary from church to church. You should follow that which is usually used in your church.

◈ The preparation

As the priest reaches the altar, bow or genuflect (page 36).
The crucifer puts the cross where it is to remain throughout
the service. Acolytes put their candles in position and go to
their places.

◈ The Greeting

◈ Collect for Purity

◈ Prayers of penitence

The prayers of penitence may be said here or after the
Intercession. The confession is said standing, but with heads
bowed.

◈ Kyrie Eleison

This is a prayer for God's mercy, used at certain seasons.
It has been used in Christian worship from very early days
and was originally in Greek. There are several versions of the
Kyries that may be used in the Eucharist.

❖ Gloria in Excelsis

The Gloria is a hymn written in the fifth century to express joy at the birth of Christ. It is omitted during Advent and Lent and on most weekdays.

❖ The Collect

This prayer 'collects' together the theme of the Eucharist and presents it as a petition to God. Before the collect a brief silence may be kept and the server should lead the people in the response, "Amen".

You may need to bring the book in which the collect is written to the priest. If there is no lectern, you may have to hold the book.

❖ The Ministry of the Word

Listen carefully to the readings. It is God who is speaking to us through his Word.

❖ Old Testament reading

❖ Psalm

❖ New Testament reading (Epistle)

Psalm, hymn or Gospel acclamation

The Old and New Testament readings are normally read by a lay person. During a weekday Eucharist the server may be required to lead the psalm and the Gospel acclamation.

During the psalm, hymn or Gospel acclamation, incense may be put on ready for the Gospel procession.

The reading of the Gospel is a focus point in the service because it is a proclaiming of the Good News of Jesus Christ to his people. This is why the book from which the Gospel is read is solemnly carried to a point in the church where this is effectively symbolised.

The Gospel reader should be accompanied by the MC (thurifer) and acolytes carrying lighted candles.

 ## The sermon

After the Gospel the servers return to their seats.
The sermon or homily that follows will normally be an attempt to explain the meaning of the readings and how to relate them to our lives. Try to set an example by listening attentively.

⊰◈⊱ The Nicene Creed

Having listened to God's Word, we now state publicly the main beliefs of our faith. It is customary to bow the head slightly at the words 'by the power of the Holy Spirit … and was made man'.

⊰◈⊱ Intercessions and thanksgivings

Servers remain standing throughout the Intercession. (Prayer of humble access)

⊰◈⊱ The peace

We exchange a greeting because we want to acknowledge publicly that Christians should be at peace with one another in unity and fellowship.

The priest may give you a peace greeting, but don't wait for him. With a handshake or handclasp greet your fellow server and say to them,

'Peace be with you, [N]',

using their Christian name. The reply may be,

'And also with you, [N]',

using your name.

You may exchange a peace greeting with other servers, choir and members of the congregation, but make sure you do not delay the start of the next part of the Eucharist.

 The preparation of the gifts

A hymn may be sung at this point, but servers should concentrate on what is happening in the sanctuary.

It is usual for bread and wine to be brought to the altar by members of the congregation at a sung Eucharist. This represents the sharing of the whole worshipping community in what is happening. You may assist the priest in receiving these gifts; and should you be given a number for communicants, mention this to him. If necessary you will need to bring the chalice and ciborium from the credence table and be ready with the wafer box if this is required. On weekdays you may need to count the congregation. Remember that the bread is to become the Body of Christ.

You then bring the water and wine cruets. Make sure the stoppers are removed. The wine will later become the Blood of Christ and the water represents ourselves. This is a sign of the coming together of the human and the divine.

It may be necessary for you to bring the alms dishes with money to the priest at this point.

Incense may now be used. If you are to be censed, bow slightly to the thurifer before and after censing. Servers and choir should be censed together, not individually.

You now bring water, a dish and a towel so that the priest may wash his fingers. A bow to the priest after the lavabo will signify that all has been completed. The priest will return the bow to indicate that he is ready to continue with the service. There is no need for conversation.

As the priest offers up the gifts of bread and wine, the server leads the response to any prayers that may be used.

The Eucharistic Prayer

The word 'Eucharist' comes from the Greek meaning 'Thanksgiving'. It indicates we are going to do what Christ did; this is: 'taking bread he gave thanks'. The central point is the Consecration – our sacrifice of praise – when the bread and wine truly become the body and blood of Jesus Christ.

The Eucharistic Prayer is at the heart of what we do in this service. Through the words and actions in which we share, Jesus Christ becomes present for us in the way he said he would at the Last Supper. It is important to remember that we have our part to play in this as well as the priest, and that the bread and wine on the altar become truly the Body and Blood of Christ.

At the elevation of the consecrated bread and wine, bells may be rung and the holy Sacrament censed.

After the priest has received Holy Communion you will receive the Sacrament (unless you are not a communicant, in which case you will be given a blessing). Each one of us should do all we can to prepare for our Communion, so that we may be worthy to share in it at every Eucharist we attend. There is no need to kneel. It is often better to receive the Sacrament standing. But you must observe the custom of your church.

It is a good custom to make the sign of the cross before you receive the Sacrament (to remind yourself that you are a disciple of Jesus Christ) and to genuflect before you return to your place (to reverence the Body and Blood of Our Lord).

◈ The distribution of Holy Communion

When there are large numbers to receive Holy Communion, the time can often seem very long. Do resist the temptation to distract one another! Instead, talk to God in your own words about the week that is over or the week that is just beginning. Pray for your family and friends, for your parish, its priest and people; or pray about something which the priest spoke of in the sermon.

There are also some prayers on page 47.

Should the Sacrament by any chance run short, be ready with wafer box or cruets, or the key for the tabernacle or aumbry, should the priest decide to use the reserved Sacrament.

After the distribution has finished, the priest will need water to cleanse the vessels and his fingers. Where and when this is done will vary according to the service or the church.

The vessels may be cleansed at a credence table. If they are cleansed at the altar, be ready to take them off when the priest has finished.

If the post-communion prayers are to be said from the lectern or from the priest's chair, make sure the appropriate book is ready where it is needed.

≋◈≋ After Communion

Here an appropriate sentence or hymn may be sung. Silence may be kept at this time, for which you should sit. If it is a long silence, remember to sit still so as not to distract others. This is a time for prayer and thanksgiving.

≋◈≋ Post-Communion prayer

≋◈≋ Blessing

≋◈≋ Dismissal

If there is a procession out, the same order is followed as the procession to the altar. Make sure all reverence the altar together.

After the service there will be further responsibilities for the server.

Try to be quiet in the sacristy. There may be a prayer. Before disrobing, vessels, cruets and books should be cleared away, candles put out and the altar left tidy.

Then we must make sure we give thanks to God for the privilege of receiving Holy Communion and assisting in the

Eucharist. We go out into the world in the joy of having served Christ. Now we must continue to serve him in the way we live and the way we serve others.

Some prayers suitable for use during the week can be found on the following pages.

Prayers

Prayer of offering

LORD Jesus,
  I give you my hands to do your work.
  I give you my feet to go your way.
  I give you my eyes to see as you do.
  I give you my tongue to speak your words.
  I give you my mind that you may think in me.
  I give you my spirit that you may pray in me.
Above all
  I give you my heart that you may love in me,
  your Father, and all mankind.
  I give you my whole self that you may grow in me,
  so that it is you. LORD Jesus,
  who live and work and pray in me.
  God be in my head, and in my understanding
  God be in mine eyes, and in my looking
  God be in my mouth, and in my speaking
  God be in my heart, and in my thinking
  God be at my end, and at my departing.

Book of Hours (1514) 40

To grow nearer to God

Day by day,
O Lord,
three things I pray;
to see thee more clearly,
love thee more dearly,
follow thee more nearly,
day by day. Amen.

St Richard of Chichester (d. 1283)

Prayer after Communion

LORD, may the Sacrament we have taken
revive us with food for the Spirit
and support us with bodily help.
Through Christ our Lord.

Roman Missal

When distracted

O LORD, take away all coldness,
all wanderings of the thoughts,
and fix our soul upon thee and thy love,
O merciful LORD, Saviour, in this our hour of prayer.

Edward W. Benson (1829-96)

For Christian witness

Guide me, teach me, strengthen me,
till I become such a person as thou wouldst have me be,
pure and gentle, truthful and high-minded,
brave and able, courteous and generous,
dutiful and useful.

Charles Kingsley (1819-1875)

For ourselves and other people

I hand over to your care, LORD,
    my soul and body,
    my mind and thoughts,
    my prayers and my hopes,
    my health and my work,
    my life and my death,
    my parents and my family,
    my friends and my neighbours,
    my country and all men,
Today and always.

Lancelot Andrewes (1555-1626)

Love of God

LORD Jesus, you have taught us that love is the fulfilling
of the law. Teach us now what love really is, how much it
costs, how far it leads, how deep it digs into our selfish
selves. Then give us the courage and the generosity to
accept what this means today and tomorrow and in the
whole future way of our lives.

Michael Hollings

In time of temptation

Help me, LORD, or I shall perish.
LORD Jesus, stiller of storms, bring peace to my soul.
LORD Jesus, I want to please thee rather than to sin,
and if I do not feel that I want to please thee,
give me the grace to want to please thee.
I *want* to want to please thee... and I do not want to sin.

Hubert van Zeiler, OSB

Act of contrition

O my God, because you are so good,
I am very sorry that I have sinned against you
and by the help of your grace I will try not to sin again.

Jesus I love you because you love me.
I am sorry I have been selfish and let you down.
Help me to answer your love with mine.

Michael Hollings

Joy in forgiveness

Happy the man whose offence is forgiven,
whose sin is remitted.
O happy the man to whom the Lord
imputes no guilt,
in whose spirit is no guile.

Psalm 31

Before study

O GOD, who hast ordained that whatever is to be desired should be sought by labour, and who, by thy blessing, bringest honest labour to good effect, look with mercy upon my studies and endeavours. Grant me, O LORD, only what is lawful and right, and afford me calmness of mind, and steadiness of purpose, so that I may so do thy will in this short life, as to obtain happiness in the world to come, for the sake of Jesus Christ our Lord.

Samuel Johnson (1709-84)

In coldness of heart

O my sweet Saviour Christ, which in thine undeserved love towards mankind, so kindly wouldst suffer the painful death of the cross, suffer me not to be cold nor lukewarm in love again towards thee.

St Thomas More (1478-1535)

For sharing

Make us worthy, LORD,
> to serve our fellow men throughout the world
> who live and die in poverty and hunger.
Give them through our hands this day their daily bread,
> and by our understanding love,
> give peace and joy.

Mother Teresa of Calcutta

In worry

O LORD, we know we very often worry about things that may never happen. Help us to live one day at a time, and to live it for you, for your name's sake.

Beryl Bye

For perseverance

O LORD, support us all the day long
    until the shades lengthen and the evening comes,
and the busy world is hushed, and the fever of life is over,
    and our work is done.
Then, LORD, in thy mercy, grant us a safe lodging,
    a holy rest, and peace at the last.
Amen.

John Henry Newman (1801-1890)

Love for others

LORD, make me an instrument of your peace:
    where there is hatred let me sow love,
    where there is injury let me sow pardon,
    where there is doubt let me sow faith,
    where there is despair let me give hope,
    where there is darkness let me give light,
    where there is sadness let me give joy.
O Divine Master, grant that I may
    not try to be comforted but to comfort,
    not try to be understood but to understand,
    not try to be loved but to love.

Because it is in giving that we receive,
    it is in forgiving that we are forgiven,
    and it is in dying that we are born to eternal life.

St Francis of Assisi (1182-1226)

Evening prayer

Receive, O LORD, our prayers and works of this day,
and grant us rest, so that we may serve you
    with renewed fervour.

Save us, O LORD, while waking,
    and guard us while sleeping,
that when we wake, we may watch with Christ,
    and when we sleep, we may rest in peace.

Roman Breviary

Joy in thanksgiving

O be joyful in the Lord, all the earth;
serve the Lord with gladness
 and come before his presence with a song.

Know that the Lord is God;
it is he that has made us and we are his;
 we are his people and the sheep of his pasture.

Enter his gates with thanksgiving
 and his courts with praise;
give thanks to him and bless his name.

For the Lord is gracious;
his steadfast love is everlasting,
 and his faithfulness endures from generation
 to generation.

Psalm 100

The Blessed Sacrament

Lord Jesus Christ,
we thank you that in this wonderful sacrament
you have given us the memorial of your passion:
 grant us so to reverence the sacred mysteries
 of your body and blood
that we may know within ourselves
 and show forth in our lives
the fruit of your redemption,
for you are alive and reign, now and for ever.

Common Worship 2000

Evening Prayer

This is the evening prayer of the Church. On Sundays it may be *solemn*, when the priest wears a cope and incense may be used. In this case a full team of servers will be required. A simple Evensong needs only one server, who will carry the cross and see to the needs of the officiant (who may not always be a priest).

Preparations

If it is to be used, the lectern needs to be prepared with the correct books for the officiant.

- ❖ If the office is sung from a stall or prayer desk, again correct books and places need to be found.

- ❖ Check that there is adequate seating for officiant and servers.

- ❖ If the preacher is a priest or deacon, there should be a stole in the pulpit before the service begins unless he is going to wear it throughout the Office.

- ❖ The candles are lit (see page 23).

The Office

The entrance procession is similar to the beginning of the Eucharist (page 37).

❖ If incense is used, the thurifer presents the thurible to the priest at the beginning of the Magnificat. After the altar and officiant have been censed, the thurifer censes the people.

❖ It is customary for the acolytes to stand by the lectern during the Creed, holding their candles for the versicles and responses and for the collects.

❖ There is no need for altar candles to be extinguished after the third collect. They should stay alight until the end of the service.

Thurible

This is used to contain the burning charcoal on which incense is put. Incense has been used since early times to honour people and things.

Incense Boat

So called because it is in the shape of a boat, and is used to hold the incense grains.

Benediction or Devotions

The service takes its name from *benedicere* which means *to bless*. In the middle of the service the priest or deacon blesses the people with the consecrated Host. The service is sometimes called *Devotions* from *Devotions to the Blessed Sacrament*.

Preparations

A cope needs to be made ready and the thurible prepared. Acolytes' candles may be required.

✤ The monstrance (if used) should be on the altar, to one side, and the tabernacle key available.
  Other preparations at the altar will include lighting candles (extra ones may be required) and arranging the corporal on which the monstrance is to be placed.

✤ If the humeral veil is needed it should be put near the altar.

The service

On entering, all genuflect and kneel. The priest exposes the Sacrament, a hymn is sung, he puts incense in the thurible and then censes the Sacrament.

❖ Devotional prayers or readings now follow; and during the hymn 'Therefore we before him bending' incense is put in the thurible and used as before.

❖ After the collect, the priest may want to put on the humeral veil (which is fastened with a clip). He then blesses the people with the Blessed Sacrament and all bow in adoration. As this happens, the bell is rung and the Sacrament is censed by the thurifer.

❖ All leave after the priest has returned the Sacrament to the tabernacle.

Monstrance

This word comes from the word *monstrare*, which means to *show*. It is the vessel in which the priest puts the consecrated Host, so that it may be seen by all the people.

Baptism

More and more, Baptism is taking place during the Eucharist or during Evensong. Baptism is initiation into the Christian life, so it makes sense that this should be done when the Christian Community is gathered together. It is most appropriate therefore that this sacrament should be administered at the main Sunday service. The servers can play their part in adding to the importance of the occasion by making sure everything is ready, and by assisting the priest at the time of the baptism.

This will take place either at the font (in which case it might be appropriate to have a small procession there to add dignity to the event) or at the chancel steps, where a bowl or a portable font will be required.

Preparations

In the Sacristy. The register for the priest to sign should be made ready, and the baptism certificates should be to hand. If several are to be baptised and the priest needs a list of names, this can be prepared by a server from the register.

At the font. Make sure there is water either in the font or in the font ewer ready to be poured. If the water can be warmed in winter, this will be a great consolation to the child! If the priest anoints and gives a baptismal candle, the oil of baptism and the unlit candle need to be at hand. The priest will also want a cloth to wipe the head of the newly baptised child (or adult), and a book containing the baptism service. Candles at the font should be lit beforehand; chiefly the Paschal candle, which is placed there after Pentecost and should have a position of prominence.

The Service

At a Eucharist the Baptism will follow the sermon, where it will take the place of the Creed and the Intercessions. The Eucharist will continue with the Peace.

❖ At Evensong the Baptism may follow the second reading.

❖ At least one server goes to the font with the priest. They should stand where they can hand the priest the holy oil and where they can take the baptismal candle, which they hand to the priest lit. They must make sure nothing falls into the water! If the certificate of baptism is to be handed out at this point, the server should see to it.

The Marriage Service

A wedding is an occasion of great joy. If a server is required, they should help to make sure all runs smoothly. The greatest need for a server will be at a wedding Eucharist (Nuptial Mass) which is how the marriage of two confirmed and communicant Christians should always be celebrated.

Preparations

A white stole will be needed for the priest, and possibly a white cope. If there is a Nuptial Mass, full vestments for a Eucharist should be set out and the altar and cruets, etc, prepared. The registers must be set out and opened either in the sacristy or on a table in the church. In church, kneelers and seats for bride and bridegroom will be needed at the chancel steps or in front of the altar, and a small dish will be required on which to place the wedding rings while they are blessed.

❖ Don't forget to light the altar candles.

❖ Books will be required for the priest as well as for the bride and groom and the bridal party. These should be to hand for the priest to see to.
  The book of readings should be ready on the lectern, or wherever is appropriate.

The service

If it is the custom in your parish, you may meet the bride at the church door with the priest and go slowly in procession up the aisle. If there is a Nuptial Mass, the wedding will take place after the sermon or homily. In other respects this is a perfectly straightforward Eucharist and normally there will be a general Communion. It will be helpful if you can get an estimate of the number wanting to receive Holy Communion.

The Funeral Service

The celebration of Christian death must convey the fact that death is not the end of life. At the same time we should be prepared to expect those who are bereaved to express their grief at a funeral service. A Requiem Eucharist should be the normal way to celebrate the funeral of a practising Christian. Do not be surprised if relatives do not understand this and opt for something more simple. We all need to be sensitive towards those who have experienced a loss.

Preparations

Make sure there is plenty of room in the front of the church for the coffin, allowing room for those who are carrying it to turn round. Put out trestles for the coffin if this is the custom in your church.

❧ A pall is a large purple cloth which may be used to cover the coffin. Have this to hand if it is to be used. It is usually needed if the coffin is brought into church to remain overnight.

❧ It is customary to place candles, either the paschal candle or other candles, near the coffin. This expresses our belief that death means sharing the life of the risen Christ.

- ❖ Symbol's of Christ's Living Word (the Bible) and his love for us (a crucifix) may be placed on the coffin during the service.

- ❖ Holy water may be needed, and incense may be used. Purple, black, or white vestments will be required. If there is a Requiem, all preparations for a Eucharist will need to be made.

The service

You may accompany the priest when the coffin is met at the church door. Holy water may be needed at this point. If it is used, it is sprinkled over the coffin to remind us that the deceased is a baptised Christian. The server may lead the procession with the cross.

A Requiem will be like any other Eucharist until near the end. After the post-Communion it is usual to say some final prayers at the coffin. Here, holy water and incense may be used.

- ❖ When the priest leaves the church for the burial or cremation, they may need to leave behind the chasuble or cope, and they may need a cloak or overcoat if the weather is bad. Do make sure they have any book they will require for the committal.